Mad Scientists

WITHDRAWN

by

Gill Arbuthnott

Illustrated by Mike Phillips

For Bruntsfield Primary School –
Thank you!

You do not need to read this page –
just get on with the book!

First published in 2008 in Great Britain by
Barrington Stoke Ltd
18 Walker St, Edinburgh, EH3 7LP

www.barringtonstoke.co.uk

ISBN: 978-1-84299-534-1

Printed in Great Britain by Bell & Bain Ltd

Contents

Intro

Science, isn't it dull? It just sits there in text books, waiting for exams. It's all been there forever, right?

Wrong! Science is done by people. Real people. And they get angry and fed-up, happy and puzzled just like everyone else.

Some of them are, or were, sensible and steady people who carefully worked out something new about science. Others were totally mad. Of course, if you discover something really important, they call this being "brilliant" instead of being mad.

Here are some of the scientist stories I like best. They're all true. Hope you enjoy them.

P.S. Lots of the scientists have names that are hard to read. Don't let that put you off. After all, this is one book about science that you won't be tested on!

Chapter 1
The Stone of Ever-lasting Life

Sir Isaac Newton (1642-1727)

You might have heard of Newton. He's famous for finding out about gravity. The force of gravity is what holds us down on the ground, even though we are whizzing round at about 1,000km an hour as the Earth spins. It's what makes us hit the ground with a thud when we fall over, and is the reason why it's not a good idea to jump out of a plane with no parachute.

A lot of people think that only big things like planets have gravity, but everything does. Small things only have a tiny bit of gravity. For example, this book is trying to pull you into its pages, but it can't do it – it's too small. And you are pulling it towards you, even when it's just sitting on the table in front of you.

The well-known story about Newton is that he was looking at an apple tree one day and saw an apple fall off it. He started to think about why an apple (or anything else) falls down instead of up. He worked out that a big thing (like the earth) pulls small things (like apples, or us) towards it. This is the force of gravity. Newton also thought that if this force went as far as the top of a tree, it might go further. In fact, it might go all the way into space. He was right. It's gravity that keeps the moon going round the earth, instead of just slipping away.

Newton was interested in lots of other things apart from gravity. He was fantastic at maths, but one of the things he liked best was alchemy.

Alchemy was a very popular hobby when Newton was alive. It was a cross between chemistry and magic, and lots of people spent their time and money on it.

They were trying to make something called the Philosopher's Stone. (No, gravity hasn't pulled you into the pages of Harry Potter, though books as big as that must have quite a lot of gravity ...)

The Philosopher's Stone was thought to let you change any metal into gold, and make you live forever. Pretty useful, for a rock.

As you might guess, no one, not even Newton, was ever able to make the Stone. Or maybe they've just kept very, very quiet about it? There is one odd fact about Newton's career which would make sense if he had found how to change metal, like lead, into gold. He was made Director of the Mint for England. This means he was in charge of all England's stores of gold. A strange job to give a scientist ...

Newton often kept secrets for years. Once, when he couldn't work something out using normal maths, he invented a new kind of maths, called Calculus, all by himself, then didn't bother to tell anyone else about it for 27 years. Calculus is very important. It lets you work out complex things like areas under curves and rates of change. So keeping it secret all that time was not a good idea.

Newton even stuck a needle in his eye (don't try this at home!) just to see what would happen. He stuck it in at the side of his eyeball until he got to the bone and wiggled it around a bit.

Wiggle!

Chapter 2
The Secret Life of Lemmings

Ole Worm (1588-1654)

You say his name 'Olay Vurm', though it sounds much funnier if you don't ...

What a daft name! I'd have wanted to put him in the book just for that, though it's probably not so funny if you're from Denmark, which he was.

Ole was interested in all kinds of animals, real or not. He was the first person to work out that the 'unicorn horns', that some people had on show in their homes back then, were nothing of the sort. They were really narwhal tusks.

Narwhals are a kind of whale. One of their teeth grows into a single tusk about 1.5 metres long. They use it to tell them about the weather. If fishermen caught narwhals they used to sell the tusks as unicorn horns for huge sums of money. Queen Elizabeth I was given one that cost £10,000. That's what a small castle cost in those days!

Ole's other big discovery was that lemmings don't appear just by falling out of the sky.

Lemmings are small, fat animals that live in Northern Europe. They look a bit like mini guinea pigs with orange, black and white fur. People used to think that they appeared just by falling out of the sky, and that they threw

themselves off cliffs in years when there were too many of them, so that the others wouldn't starve.

Of course, they don't do this. What happens is that in years when they have lots of babies, they eat up all the food where they live. A crowd of them set off to find food somewhere else. They run after each other in a big bunch, and sometimes some of them fall off cliffs or into rivers. Because they're all running so close together, quite a lot fall to their deaths before they can stop.

But why would anyone think they fell out of the sky?

People had some funny ideas about where animals came from in those days. They thought that mud turned into swallows, and that oil could turn into snakes. If you wanted some mice (I don't know why you would, but anyway ...) all you had to do was put a handful of seeds and an old shirt on the floor of a barn over-night, and in the morning – mice! Amazing!

Ole was the first person to work out that:

Boy Lemming + Girl Lemming = Baby Lemmings

It was an odd thing but he still believed all the stuff about snakes and mud and mice. It would be another 200 years before a different scientist, called Louis Pasteur, showed that it was all nonsense ...

Chapter 3
Eggs on Toast
Rita Levi-Montalcini (1909 - Now)

Rita Levi-Montalcini was born in Italy. Her father made her leave her normal school and go to one that would teach her to be a 'good wife'. She hated it because she didn't learn anything she thought was useful. Instead, she got lessons in cooking and cleaning and how to make her house look nice.

By the end of her time there, Rita had made up her mind that she wanted to be a doctor. In the end she was able to talk her father into letting her study medicine.

When she finished, she didn't know whether to become a doctor or do research, but in 1938 Mussolini, the Italian ruler, said that Jewish people couldn't teach, be doctors, or work in a university.

Rita tried to be a doctor helping poor people anyway, but because she was Jewish, she wasn't allowed to order medicines, so it didn't work.

Instead, she set up a secret lab in her bedroom, and started to study how nerve cells grow. She couldn't get proper equipment, so she made tiny tools herself out of sewing needles. She worked on eggs, and when she finished an experiment, she would always cook and eat what was left. No one wasted food during the war.

The family had to keep moving house so they couldn't be arrested and sent to death camps in Nazi Germany. They used fake

identity papers made by Rita and her sister. They all lived through the war.

After the war, Rita worked in America for many years. She discovered an important chemical that is needed for nerve cells to grow. This was so important that she won the Nobel Prize for Medicine in 1986. She kept doing research until she was more than 80 years old.

She is still alive. In fact, she is the oldest living Nobel Prize winner.

Chapter 4
The Human Test Tube
Alexis St Martin (1794-1880)

This is a bit of a cheat. Alexis St Martin wasn't a scientist, he was an experiment. Let me explain ...

Alexis came from Canada. He had a job collecting furs from animal-trappers. In 1822, he was shot by mistake. Oops! He lost some ribs, a bit of a lung, and a big lump of his chest wall. When it got better, he was left with a hole in his chest, big enough to stick a finger into. It went all the way into his stomach! This made eating a bit messy, as the food fell out of the hole unless it was bandaged up.

Doctor Beaumont, who had treated Alexis, started to do experiments on him. The doctor hung bits of food on threads and poked them into Alexis's stomach. After a

few hours he would pull them out again to
see what had happened to them. He tried
lots of different foods to find out which ones
were hard to digest, and which were easy.
He also stuck a thermometer into the hole to
find out what temperature it was inside the
stomach.

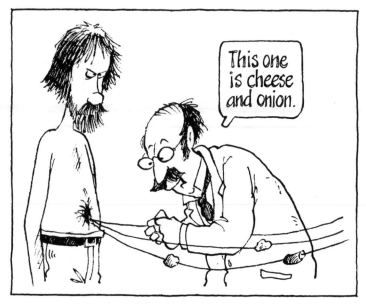

In the end, Alexis got a bit fed up (ha ha)
with this, and went off to get married and
try to live a more normal life. However, he
came back to Doctor Beaumont after a few

years, and let him do more experiments while he worked for the doctor as an odd job man. The doctor did experiments on him for 8 years, and found out more than anyone else then knew about how the stomach breaks down food.

Alexis lived until he was 86. Not bad for a man with a hole in his chest. When he died, his family thought that other scientists might want to cut his body up to do more experiments on it. To stop this happening, they left his body in the sun for four days, so it started to rot. Then they dug a hole and buried him in secret. They didn't put a grave stone up to mark where it was.

The family kept the grave secret for years. It wasn't until 1962 that one of his grand-daughters, who was now an old woman, told people where it was. When they found out, they put up a sign on the church wall near the grave so people would know how much Alexis had helped science.

Chapter 5

One Cat – Dead or Alive

Erwin Schrödinger (1887-1961)

I know – another daft name. Why can't any of these people be called John Smith?

I don't know if Erwin had a pet cat, but if he did, it must have spent a lot of time worrying. Here's why.

Erwin thought up the most famous experiment that's never been done. Yes, you did read that properly! I think you have to be an expert to understand the point of an experiment that was never carried out, but it's so crazy, I had to put it in here.

Let's think of it as a cooking recipe ...

Dead and Alive Cat

<u>Ingredients</u>

One cat

One big, sound-proof metal box

One bit of radio-active stuff

One radio-activity detector

One hammer

One bottle of poison gas

Method

Put the radio-active stuff at one end of the box, with the detector near it.

Put the hammer and poison near them, so that if the hammer falls, it breaks open the bottle of poison.

Fix the hammer to the detector, so that if any radio-activity comes out of the radio-active stuff, it sets the detector off and makes the hammer fall.

Add the cat and shut the box.

Wait for an hour.

The radio-active stuff has a 50:50 chance of setting off the detector in an hour, so the cat has a 50:50 chance of staying alive. You don't know if it's alive or dead unless you open the box.

Still with me? Oh, good. The next bit is where I get very confused.

Erwin went on to argue that the cat could be alive or dead, but until you open the box, you don't know which. OK, that sounds sensible. But then he said that until you open the box, the cat isn't alive or dead, but somehow both at the same time. (No, I don't understand that bit either.) By opening the box you force it to be one thing or the other. I understand that this all makes perfect sense if you are into Quantum Physics.

Of course, those of us who own a cat know that if it was still alive, it would rip your face off as it jumped out of the box hissing ...

P.S. Don't try this at home!

Chapter 6

The Dinosaur Detectives

No one has ever seen a dinosaur, but we all know what they look like. Or at least, we think we do.

Who were the people who first found the fossils that showed that dinosaurs had existed? Who were the people who gave them their names and worked out what they looked like?

And what has this got to do with one of the most crazy dinner parties ever held?

Read on ...

William Buckland (1784-1856)

Buckland was a professor at Oxford University. He was very interested in fossils, and in trying to work out the age of the earth. He also had some very strange hobbies.

He kept lots of animals in his home, including a family of guinea pigs that were allowed to wander round the rooms. That was fine, until he got a pet jackal (it's a sort of wild dog). Not many of the guinea pigs lived after that, and visitors complained that they had to put their feet up on the chairs so they weren't bitten by the jackal!

He also had a pet bear, which was very tame. He had a set of clothes made for it, so it could join in with student life. He even took it to parties with him. It liked wine parties most of all.

One of the things he set out to do was to eat every animal there was. Visitors might find they were getting mice on toast for supper. Buckland said that he liked the taste of every animal he ate, apart from moles.

He also found an ancient hyena den, full of fossil bones. You might think this was in Africa, but it was in Yorkshire. Everyone was very surprised to find that hyenas had once lived there. Buckland showed they really had been hyenas by buying one of his own. He looked at the bite marks it left on bones and compared those marks with the ones on the bones he had found. Buckland called his pet hyena Billy. I'd love to know if Billy got eaten too!

Another of his important finds was fossil bones from an animal that was 12 metres long, which turned out to be a dinosaur.

Buckland also got very interested in strange stones with spiral marks on them that kept turning up on the beach at Lyme Bay on the south coast of England. When at last scientists worked out that it was fossil poo, work was held up for ages, because people thought it was rude to talk about it!

Buckland came to a sad end. He had always been odd, to say the least, but in 1851 he began to go mad. His family had to send him to a hospital for people who were mad. He died there in 1856.

Richard Owen (1804-1892) and Gideon Mantell (1790-1852)

These two spent much of their life working against each other, and in the end, one was to destroy the other.

Mantell was the son of a shoe-maker, with six brothers and sisters, so there wasn't very much money to be had. However, his uncle ran a school so he was able to go there without having to pay.

He trained as a doctor and started work as a surgeon in the south of England, but his real interest was fossil hunting. He found a number of huge fossil bones, and worked out how big the animals would have been when they were alive. They were so big that almost no one would believe he was right. He went on working on the fossils anyway and wrote scientific papers about them.

Mantell and his family never had quite enough money. They moved to Brighton, hoping that lots of rich people would want him as their doctor. (There was no National Health Service then. In those days, if you wanted a doctor, you had to pay.) Mantell also opened a fossil museum in his house. His wife began to get a bit fed up with so many visitors. The museum was a big success, but not many people wanted a doctor who was more interested in fossils than sick people ...

Owen also trained as a surgeon. He got obsessed with anatomy. (That's learning about bodies by cutting them up.) Once he stole the head of a dead body he had been working on in a prison, and took it home. On the way he slipped on ice and dropped the head. It rolled down a hill and into a cottage! The people in the village thought they were being haunted by a ghost.

Owen moved to London, where he became very successful. Any animal from London Zoo that died was sent to him to study. Sent to his house. Yes, really. Once, he came home to find a dead rhino in his hall!

Owen came up with a catchy name for the giant fossil lizards. He called them dinosaurs. Owen wanted to be the top expert in the country, and he began to see Mantell as someone who might get in his way.

When Mantell's money ran out, he had to sell his house and move into rented rooms. In the end, he had to sell all his fossils, something he said was like 'selling his children'. Even worse, his wife got fed up and left him. He had lost everything.

By this time Owen was getting to be more and more successful, but he cheated. He claimed the research that people like Mantell and Buckland had done years before as his own work. He even tried to stop the Royal Society in London from giving Mantell a special medal for all his work on fossils.

Mantell moved to London and tried to restart his medical career. In 1841 his life got even worse. He fell from a coach in an accident and got dragged behind it. From then on, he was in constant pain and could hardly walk.

Mantell died alone and in pain in 1852. His spine, twisted by the accident, was put on show in the museum of the Royal College of Surgeons, which was run by – wait for it – Richard Owen! The spine was destroyed by a bomb during World War Two.

Owen was determined to get a new museum built in London, where all the dinosaur fossils could go on display. It became the Museum of Natural History. If you visit it today you can see Owen's statue at the top of the stairs.

By the time Owen died, in 1892, most of his work on fossils had been proved wrong, or just forgotten.

OK, this hasn't been very cheery, has it? Everyone ended up miserable and then dead. Even the dinosaurs. So what about this strange dinner I promised you?

Picture this. In 1851 the Crystal Palace (a huge glass building) was built in London for the Great Exhibition. This was to show how wonderful Britain was at ... well, everything really. It was a huge success, and the next year it moved to a new home in another part of London. There was only one thing missing – dinosaurs. The biggest and best of everything else was on show, so they wanted the biggest and best animals too – or at least, life-sized models.

Mantell was asked to be in charge of this, but he was dying. Guess who took over? Yes, it was Owen. Hollow concrete models of all the dinosaurs were made, and set in among the trees and bushes, as people thought they would have looked.

The biggest model was over 10 metres long. Before the top was put on it, a dinner party was held in the belly of the beast. 21 people were there on New Year's Eve 1853. They had an 8-course meal, and fine wines. Mantell wasn't there. He had died the month before.

The models are still there today, chipped and unloved. No one seems to care about them any more, or know why they're there. But you do.

Chapter 7

Oops! or It Seemed Like a Good Idea at the Time ...

Thomas Midgely (1889-1944)

People can't always predict what will happen as a result of something they've done. Here is a spectacular example.

Thomas Midgely was a chemist from America. In 1921 he invented something called tetraethyl lead. He found out that it made car engines run more smoothly, and from then on, it was added to petrol. Now that's great if you're a car, but not so good for living things – humans, for example. Lead is deadly. It messes up your brain and nervous system. The companies that made the lead compound began to notice that their workers were getting ill, and sometimes dying. Did they stop making it? Of course not! It was worth too much money to stop.

In fact, lead was still in most petrol until a few years ago. We're getting rid of the stuff now though, thank goodness.

Thomas Midgely invented something else. This was a special gas to put in the cooling systems of fridges. It's got a long name, but people usually call it CFC. It works very well in fridges but (you know what's coming, don't you?) it's very bad for people.

Why? Well, when it escapes from the fridge (maybe when the fridge is thrown away), it floats up to the ozone layer, and gobbles it up.

This is not good. The ozone layer protects us from a lot of dangerous ultra-violet radiation. If it isn't there any more, we're more likely to get skin cancer. CFC is also one of the gases that is causing climate change.

It's hard not to think the world would have been a better place if Thomas Midgely had gone to work in a bank!

He got a disease that left him crippled, called polio – so he invented a machine to help move him around in bed. One night he got tangled up in the straps, and they choked him to death. He died before he found out how bad his inventions were. Probably just as well.

Chapter 8
The Countess of Numbers
Ada Lovelace (1815-1852)

Ada Byron was the daughter of a very
famous poet – Lord Byron. As well as being a
poet, Ada's father was famous for being a
Very Bad Man. Ada was his daughter from a
very short marriage. She never met her
father.

Her mother wanted her to be as unlike
her father as possible, so Ada was taught

maths and music to keep any risky talent as a poet from showing up.

Ada turned out to be amazing at maths. When she was only 13, she drew up a plan for a flying machine. (She didn't build it though.) She and her mother lived among rich people in London. They thought it was very odd that a rich young woman wanted to use her brain!

When Ada was 17, she met Charles Babbage, a maths professor at Cambridge University. He had invented something called the Difference Engine. This was a machine that calculated numbers, and in some ways, it was the first computer. They began to write to each other about maths and many other subjects.

When Ada was 20, she married William King, the Earl of Lovelace, so she became the Countess of Lovelace.

Babbage was planning an even more complicated machine, and Ada helped him write about it to try and get the money to build it. Although it was Babbage who drew up the plans for it, Ada understood more clearly than him how useful it might turn out to be. Her notes talk about all sorts of things that might be possible using machines like this – even electronic music! (Not that she used those words.)

Ada had a bad habit, however, which got her into a lot of trouble. She loved to gamble. In fact, once she started she couldn't stop. She thought she could work out a way to predict the results of horse races because she was so good with numbers, but it didn't work. She began to owe people a lot of money.

She died of cancer when she was 37, and was buried next to her famous father.

Chapter 9

The Man Who Weighed
the Earth

Henry Cavendish (1731-1810)

Henry Cavendish was born into a very rich family. This allowed him to spend all his time doing experiments without having to worry about money. He turned his house in London into a huge lab, and did chemistry and physics experiments there.

In one set of experiments, he gave himself electric shocks – small ones at first, then bigger ones. Some of them were big enough to knock him out!

Cavendish worked out a lot of important things, but no one knew about most of them until after he died. This was because he was very, very shy. He would sometimes run away from people who tried to talk to him.

The most amazing thing Cavendish did was to work out how heavy the Earth is. He did this in 1797. He used a very complicated machine that had been made by another scientist called John Michell.

Cavendish worked out that the Earth had a mass of 6,000,000,000,000,000,000,000,000 kg. That's six million trillion kilos (if I got the number of zeroes right).

This figure is only about 1% more than estimates made by modern scientists using the most up-to-date methods. Not bad!

Chapter 10
The Story of Evolution
Charles Darwin (1809-1882)

I'm pretty sure you'll have heard of him.
You might also know that he came up with
something called the Theory of Evolution.
You may not know what it is though, or that
Darwin felt it had ruined his life.

Darwin studied medicine in Edinburgh,
but gave it up. He tried law, but gave up that
too. He didn't seem very sure what he

wanted to do. At last, he answered an advert to go on a long trip by sea on a ship called the Beagle.

He spent five years on the ship, travelling all round the world. He was able to collect a huge number of different kinds of plants, animals and fossils to take home and study.

He found out that places with the same weather and soil didn't always have the same animals and plants. For instance, two sides of the same mountain range could have quite different plants. He couldn't work out why. If God had made everything, why wouldn't he put the same plants on both sides?

The fossils that were being collected everywhere made it look as if the animals that lived long ago were different to the ones we have now. That didn't fit with the idea of God making everything either, unless he kept changing his mind.

When he came back to Britain, Darwin also looked at the results of Artificial Selection. This is the way we've bred almost all our farm animals and plants, so that they're exactly how we want them to be. We still use it now.

Suppose you wanted to breed really fluffy kittens. You would choose the fluffiest cats you could find and let them have kittens together. Then you would pick out the fluffiest of their kittens and let them have kittens too. You would go on doing that until you had the great, great, great grand-kittens of the first two cats. If you got it right, you would now have very fluffy cats indeed.

Darwin wondered if there could be some sort of selection process going on in wild animals and plants that made them change over a very long time. Of course, it couldn't be people choosing the ones that got to have babies. It must be something else.

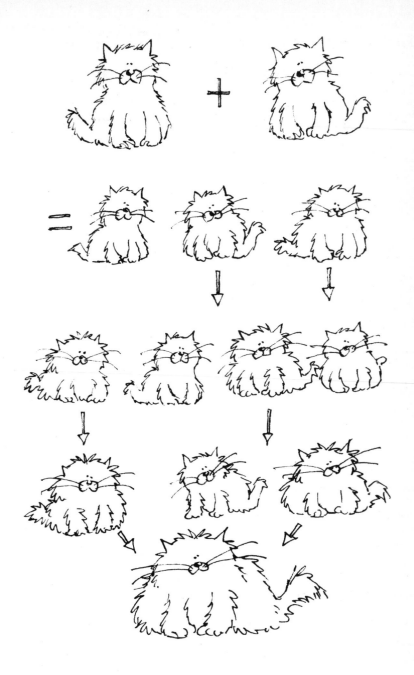

Darwin read a book by a mathematician called Malthus at about this time. It showed that no matter how many babies particular animals have, the size of the population stays about the same. For instance, one fish like a herring lays about 2,000,000 eggs. If they all survived, the sea would soon be solid herring instead of water. But they don't all survive, and that's very important.

Darwin realised that not all herring (or any other animal or plant) are the same, and that they all compete for things like food. Some herring can survive better than others. Maybe they can swim faster, or catch more food. These are the ones that live long enough to breed. The ones that are slow, or aren't good at finding food, often die before they can breed.

The best ones survive, and they pass on the things that made them the best to their babies. Slowly, more and more of them get fast, or good at hiding, until they all are. But by now these fish have also changed so much from the first herring that they count as a new species!

Over millions of years, this could explain how different kinds of animals and plants appeared.

Darwin was very upset by this. You'd think he'd be pleased, wouldn't you? Well, he wasn't. He was upset because if humans changed like this, it must mean they weren't made by God to be special, but were just like any other animal. This was a shocking idea then.

In 1844, he wrote all this down, then put the papers away in a drawer for 15 years, and worked on other things. One reason might be that someone else wrote a book on Evolution that year. It was very unpopular, and was attacked by professors and people of the church. The book was written by a man called Robert Chambers, who was a publisher. The publishing firm is still around today – you might have seen a Chambers Dictionary.

In 1858 Darwin got a letter from a man called Alfred Russell Wallace. He had come up with an idea that was almost the same as Darwin's. Their idea was presented at a scientific meeting, but no one took much notice of it!

Darwin wrote it up as a book called *On the Origin of Species*. Even then, he was so upset by what he was doing that he kept being sick when he was checking it over. He hated what he had done. He said he felt as if he was 'confessing a murder'. His wife, who was very religious, was even more upset.

In another of his books Darwin wrote about man and apes having come from the same ancestor (which wasn't man or ape)

millions of years ago. Lots of people get this wrong and think he said man was descended directly from apes.

Darwin died in 1882. The Theory of Evolution wasn't widely believed until the 1930s. Even today there are arguments about it. In the USA some school boards try to stop it from being taught.

Last Word

Well, I hope I've made you think that scientists are interesting people. There are lots more I could have written about. If you enjoyed the book, why don't you see if you can find out about some more of them? Here are two puzzles to get you started.

Who was the scientist whose cookery books still have to be kept in a metal box made of lead because they're so radio-active?

Which scientist infected a small boy with a deadly illness on purpose to see if he could make people immune to it?

Barrington Stoke would like to thank all its readers for commenting on the manuscript before publication and in particular:

Amrita Brara
Maya Brara
Barney Casserly
Mandy Peters
Sam Peters
Jamie Smith

Become a Consultant!

Would you like to give us feedback on our titles before they are published? Contact us at the email address below – we'd love to hear from you!

info@barringtonstoke.co.uk
www.barringtonstoke.co.uk

AUTHOR CHECK LIST

Gill Arbuthnott

What is the maddest thing you have ever done?

Nothing very mad ... I went out once to buy a black kitten and came back with a deaf, one-eyed white adult cat. (It wasn't my fault though: he chose me.) Oh, and there was the time at the fun fair when I went on a roller coaster even though I knew I hated them. It felt like the longest two minutes of my life.

Which of the mad scientists would you have liked to meet and why?

Rita Levi-Montalcini. Not only did she do important work under very difficult conditions, she lived through amazing times. She also had great style in the way she dressed and looked, and she was a fabulous cook. What a woman!

Which discovery would you like to have made?

I'd love to have been part of the discovery of the structure of DNA (the chemical that controls most of what we are). It's so beautiful, and it unlocked so many ideas in Biology. AND I would have got to work with some incredible people. Maybe I'll tell you about them in another book!

What do you think is the best discovery made by a scientist?

It's not an important discovery, but it has made a lot of people very happy ... The discovery of how to make chocolate so that it starts to melt at the temperature of the human mouth!

ILLUSTRATOR CHECK LIST

Mike Phillips

What is the maddest thing you have ever done?

Swimming with sharks. Exciting and very scary at the same time!

Which of the mad scientists would you have liked to meet and why?

Charles Darwin. I would have loved to have gone with him round the world, collecting all those weird and wonderful plants and animals.

What discovery would you like to have made and why?

The discovery of Penicillin. It saved so many lives.

What do you think is the best discovery made by a scientist?

The research done by Rita Levi-Montalcini. Anything to do with the improvement of human life is a great discovery.

Who would you least like to do experiments on you and why?

My three children. They would enjoy it too much.

Try another book in the
REALITY CHECK
series

The Land of Whizzing Arrows
by Simon Chapman

Pocket Hero
by Pippa Goodhart

The Last Duel
by Martyn Beardsley

Escape From Colditz
by Deborah Chancellor

Dick Turpin: Legends and Lies
by Terry Deary

Crazy Creatures
by Gill Arbuthnott